Character Education

Consideration

by Lucia Raatma

Consultant:
Madonna Murphy, Ph.D.
Associate Professor of Education
University of St. Francis, Joliet, Illinois
Author, *Character Education in America's
Blue Ribbon Schools*

Bridgestone Books
an imprint of Capstone Press
Mankato, Minnesota

Bridgestone Books are published by Capstone Press
818 North Willow Street, Mankato, Minnesota 56001
http://www.capstone-press.com

Library of Congress Cataloging-in-Publication Data
Raatma, Lucia.
    Consideration/by Lucia Raatma.
    p. cm.—(Character education)
    Includes bibliographical references and index.
    Summary: Describes consideration as the virtue of being thoughtful and
suggests ways in which consideration can be shown.
    ISBN 0-7368-0367-X
    1. Thoughtfulness—Juvenile literature. [1. Thoughtfulness.] I. Title. II. Series.
BJ1533.T45R33 2000
177'.7—dc21
                                                                    99-31307
                                                                         CIP

Editorial Credits

Christy Steele, editor; Heather Kindseth, cover designer and illustrator;
    Kimberly Danger, photo researcher

Photo Credits

Archive Photos/J.M. Ribeiro, 18
David F. Clobes, 4
Houston Deaton, 14, 16
Index Stock Imagery/David R. Frazier, 10
Marilyn Moseley La Mantia, cover
Photo Network/Myrleen Cate, 8
Photri-Microstock/Bachmann, 12
Shaffer Photography/James L. Shaffer, 6, 20

Table of Contents

Consideration

Consideration means being thoughtful of the needs and feelings of other people. Considerate people are kind and caring. They respect the rights of other people. Considerate people help others. People appreciate those who show consideration.

appreciate
to enjoy or value someone

Being Polite

Considerate people are polite to others. Using good manners is one way to be polite. Say "please" when you ask for something. Say "thank you" when others give you gifts. Compliment people when they do a good job. Listen to people without interrupting them.

compliment
to tell someone that you admire them or feel they have done something well

7

Being Considerate at Home

You can show consideration for your family in many ways. You can clean up after you play with toys. You can turn down the radio if your dad is resting. You can help your younger sister get ready for school.

Being Considerate to Friends

Being considerate is an important part of friendship. You can be considerate by meeting your friends on time. You can ask a friend to choose a movie to see. You can send a thank-you card to a friend who has helped you. Showing consideration will strengthen friendships.

Being Considerate at School

You can help others by being considerate at school. You can lend a pencil to a classmate to take a test. You can stay quiet in the library so other students can study. Raise your hand if you want to talk during class. Being considerate can make school a friendly place.

Being Considerate to Strangers

You must be careful around strangers. But you can still show consideration to them. Hold the door open for someone carrying books. You can be considerate by not talking during a movie. Wait your turn in line instead of moving ahead of others.

Being Considerate in Your Community

You can show consideration for your community in many ways. Use the sidewalk instead of walking across a neighbor's yard. Be quiet at night so neighbors can sleep. Do not litter. Considerate people make communities nice places to live.

litter
to throw garbage on the ground

"Someone has to go out there and love people."
—From an interview with Princess Diana

Princess Diana and Consideration

Diana Windsor was Princess of Wales from 1981 to 1996. She was considerate to all people. She greeted everyone she met. She visited sick people in hospitals. Princess Diana's consideration helped make people's lives better.

Consideration and You

Considerate people are thoughtful and polite. They do small things every day to show that they care for others. People you help will appreciate your thoughtfulness. Helping others will make you feel good.

Hands On: Write Thank-You Notes

The people at your school work hard to help you. Show your consideration for them by writing thank-you notes.

What You Need

envelope
paper
pen or pencil

What You Do

1. Make a list of all the workers at your school. The list may include principals, cafeteria workers, custodians, teachers, coaches, secretaries, school nurses, and bus drivers.
2. Ask each student in your class to choose a name from your list.
3. Each student should write a note to the school worker chosen. Thank the school workers for the things they do.
4. Ask your teacher to deliver the thank-you notes.

Words to Know

appreciate (uh-PREE-shee-ate)—to enjoy or value someone

compliment (KOM-pluh-ment)—to tell someone that you admire them or feel they have done something well

litter (LIT-ur)—to throw garbage on the ground

manners (MAN-urss)—polite behavior

Read More

Krohn, Katherine E. *Princess Diana.* A & E Biography. Minneapolis: Lerner Publications, 1999.

Petrucelli, Rita. *Learn the Value of Consideration.* Vero Beach, Fla.: Rourke, 1989.

Internet Sites

Adventures from the Book of Virtues Home Page
http://www.pbs.org/adventures

The Character Building Site
http://www.usoe.k12.ut.us/curr/char_ed/chbldr/
  characterbuilder.html

Character Counts! The Six Pillars of Character
http://www.charactercounts.org/defsix.htm

The Giraffe Program
http://www.giraffe.org/tall.html

Index